MICHAEL OWEN
SOCCER BOY WONDER

Alex Murphy

P

|| •PARRAGON• ||

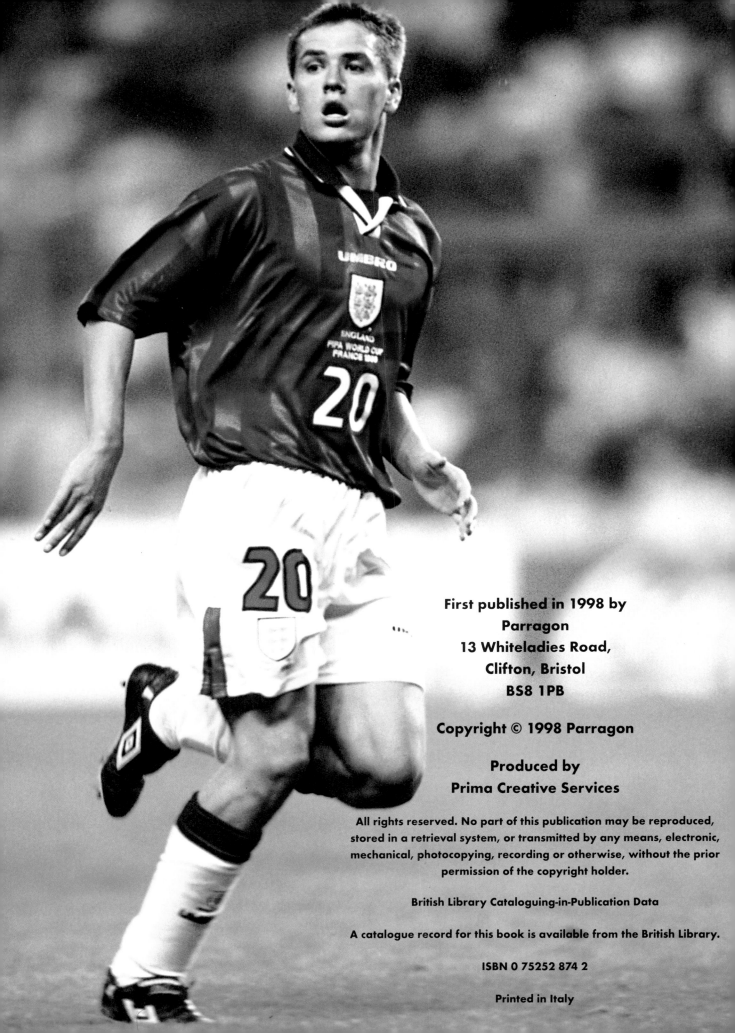

First published in 1998 by
Parragon
13 Whiteladies Road,
Clifton, Bristol
BS8 1PB

Copyright © 1998 Parragon

Produced by
Prima Creative Services

British Library Cataloguing-in-Publication Data

A catalogue record for this book is available from the British Library.

ISBN 0 75252 874 2

Printed in Italy

CONTENTS

INTRODUCTI

Most **boys** can only dream about **playing** for a big **Premiership team** when they are still just 17. And **scoring** for England in the **World Cup** when you are only 18 is an even wilder fantasy. But for **Liverpool's** brilliant young **striker**, **Michael Owen**, those **dreams** have come **true**. It seems hard to **believe** that **Michael** went from **playing** schoolboy **football** to world stardom in just a couple of years. But that is **exactly** what happened. He became a **professional** player when he graduated from **Liverpool's** junior team in **December 1996**, and just **18 months** later he was **famous** all over the **world** for his **breathtaking** displays in the **World Cup** in France, capped by one of the **best** goals the **tournament** has ever seen, against **Argentina!**

Despite all the **attention**, Michael has kept his **feet** firmly on the **ground**. Even though his **skill** has already made him a very **rich** young man, the **modest** teenager likes living **quietly** with his **family** in a village just outside **Chester**. His **coaches** at **Liverpool**, and **devoted** dad, **Terry**, a former **professional** himself, will make sure he makes the **most** of his amazing **talent**.

EARLY

It did **not** take very **long** to see that **Michael** was an exceptionally **talented** footballer. Even as a **tiny** seven-year-old, he was **playing** against boys much **bigger** than himself — and **scoring** goals.

His first **team** was called **Mold Alexandra** Under 10s, and **Michael** was **easily** their **best player**, even though

LIFE

he was by far the **youngest**. In his **first** season he **scored 34 goals** in only **28 matches** – including **nine** in just **one** game.

Next season **Michael**, now **eight**, was picked to play for the **district** team – **Deeside Primary Schools**, and word of his **goal-scoring** soon spread to **scouts** from every big **club** in the **country**. He **scored** an incredible **97 goals** for the **team**, beating a **record** previously held by another **Liverpool** legend, **Ian Rush**.

It was **no surprise** that he **soon** received **invitations** to train with League **clubs**, including **Arsenal** and **Manchester United**. But after visiting a number of them, Michael chose **Liverpool** – even though he really supported **The Reds'** deadly local rivals, **Everton!**

ENGLAN

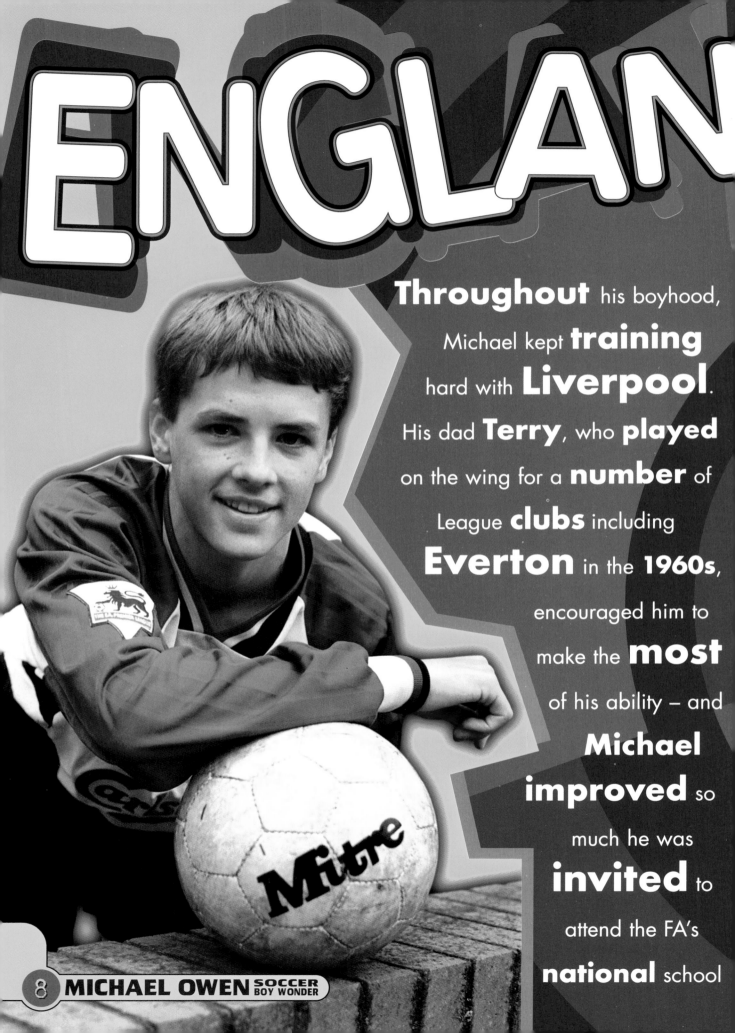

Throughout his boyhood, Michael kept **training** hard with **Liverpool**. His dad **Terry**, who **played** on the wing for a **number** of League **clubs** including **Everton** in the **1960s**, encouraged him to make the **most** of his ability – and **Michael improved** so much he was **invited** to attend the FA's **national** school

SCHOOLBOY

for **outstanding** schoolboy players at **Lilleshall**. Michael **impressed** the staff there, and he was **chosen** to play for **England Schoolboys**. In 1995/96 he carried on his **habit** of breaking **records** by scoring **12 times** for the **national** schools side. And **Liverpool** were delighted with his **progress** as he fired them to their **first-ever** triumph in the FA **Youth Cup** in 1996, scoring **11 goals** in only **five** games. It was no wonder **Liverpool** were keen to **sign** him as a full **professional** – and he joined **The Reds** officially on his 17th birthday in **December 1996**.

Even though lots of **people** said he was still too **small** and too young, the **wise** coaches at **Anfield** knew **Michael** was **ready** to make his debut for the **first team**. So on **6th May 1997**, Michael **ran** out at Selhurst Park where **Liverpool** were playing **Wimbledon**, to a roar from **The Reds'** travelling **supporters**. The frail-looking substitute was only **17** – yet **amazingly** within moments he was **already** a hero to The Reds' **fanatical** followers. He **scored** a goal just as **easily** as he used to do for **Mold Alexandra** Under 10s, and became the **youngest** player ever to score for **Liverpool**. The fans loved the **coolness** of their new **young player** – and the daring way he used his speed to **frighten** opposition defenders. Already, **supporters** were **likening** him to other great **Liverpool strikers**, like **Robbie Fowler** and **Ian Rush**.

He **finished** the 1996/97 **season** with two first-team **appearances** to his name, and **one goal**. It was just a taste of the **amazing** things which were to come in his **first** full **League campaign**.

L DEBUT

It is **hard** to think of another **player** who has made such a **dramatic** impact in their first **full** season. Before the **1997/98** campaign began, **hardly** anyone had **even** heard of **Michael**. But by the end, **he** was a **household** name, the joint **top-scorer** in the **Premier League** with **18** goals in **36** games. His **ambition** before the season had been to play a few **games** in Liverpool's **first-team**. As it turned out, he missed only **two**, forced his way into England's **World Cup squad**, was voted Carling **Player Of The Year** and the Players' **Young Player Of The Year**. He had packed more **honours** into one season than many players **achieve** in a whole career. But **Owen** had his black **moments** too. In April he

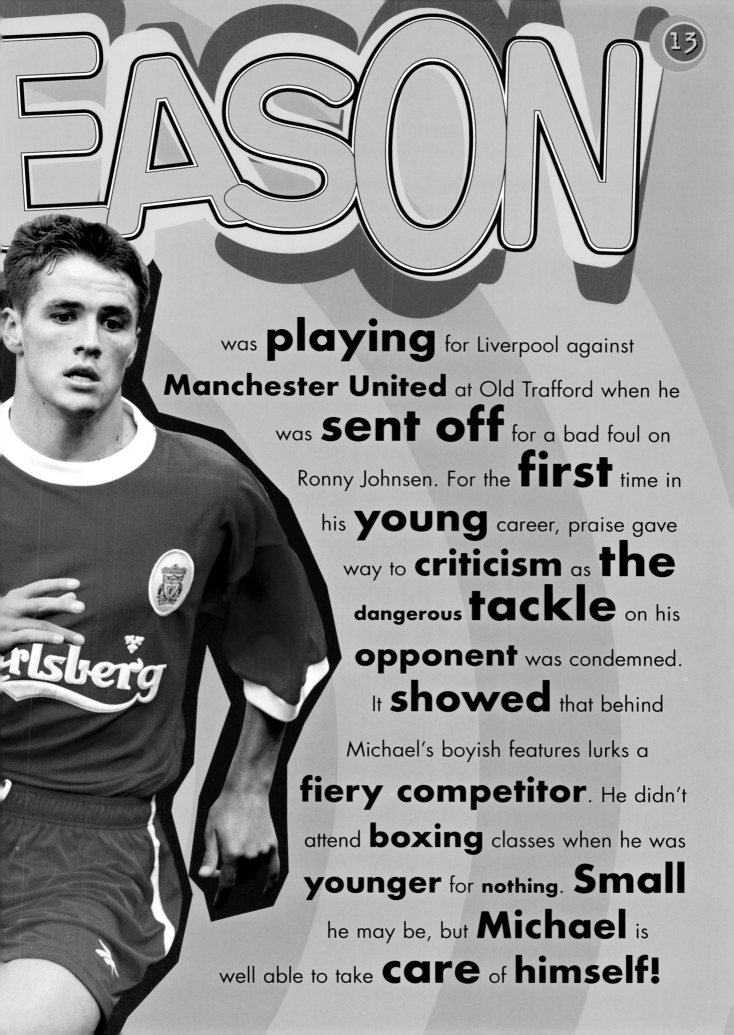

SEASON!

was **playing** for Liverpool against **Manchester United** at Old Trafford when he was **sent off** for a bad foul on Ronny Johnsen. For the **first** time in his **young** career, praise gave way to **criticism** as **the dangerous tackle** on his **opponent** was condemned. It **showed** that behind

Michael's boyish features lurks a **fiery competitor**. He didn't attend **boxing** classes when he was **younger** for **nothing**. **Small** he may be, but **Michael** is well able to take **care** of **himself!**

ENGLAND

With the goals **flying** in for **Liverpool**, Michael **quickly** caught the attention of England's coach, **Glenn Hoddle**. And on **February 11 1998** he made his **international** debut in a **friendly** against **Chile** at Wembley. Sadly **England** lost **2-0**, but **Michael** caught the eye as their **best player**. He nearly **scored** with an **early shot**, but even though he did not make the **score** sheet, Michael still made **history** – as usual! He became the **youngest** England

DEBUT

player this century at **18 years 59 days**. **Despite** his age **Michael** soon made **himself** an automatic choice for England's **World Cup** squad. He played a **full** part in the **warm-up** matches, **winning caps** against **Switzerland**, Portugal, Morocco and **Belgium**. And in the game against Morocco he **scored** his first **international goal** – breaking another **record** into the **bargain!** He became the **youngest player** ever to score for **England**.

THE WOR

When **England's** **World Cup** campaign **kicked off** in France, Michael was **left** kicking his **heels** on the **substitutes'** bench. In the opening **game** against **Tunisia**, England coach **Glen Hoddle** preferred **Teddy** **Sheringham** of Manchester United to play alongside **Alan Shearer** in attack. They **won 2-0**, and Michael only saw six minutes of **action** as he came on in place of **Sheringham**. He made a much **bigger** impression

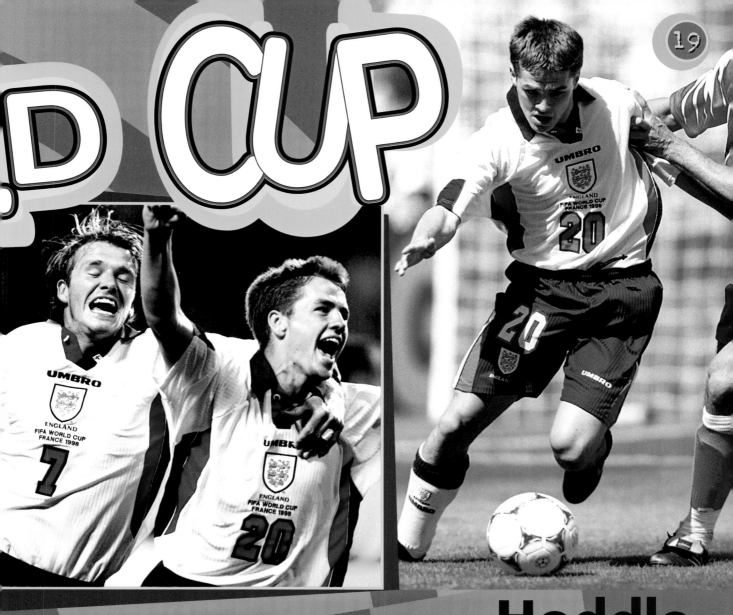

in the second match, against **Romania**. This time **Hoddle** brought him on with 17 minutes to go, when **England** were **losing 1-0**. **Michael** announced his arrival at the tournament after just **10 minutes**, poaching a **goal** to put **England** level. Romania, though, scored in the last seconds to win **2-1**. That meant **England** had to beat **Colombia** to make sure of **qualifying** for the competition's **Second Round** – and at last Michael was **promoted** to the starting team. He **played** his part in the **2-0 win** that set up the historic clash with **Argentina**.

Michael's reputation as one of the **best strikers** in the **world** was **won** mainly thanks to his **performance** in one match – **England** versus *Argentina* in the Second Round of the **World Cup** on 30th June 1998. Who can forget his **goal** after **16 minutes**, when he took on Argentina's **defence** single-handed, **dribbled** around two **world-class** players and **rocketed** an unstoppable **shot** beyond the goal-keeper's grasp? Not since the

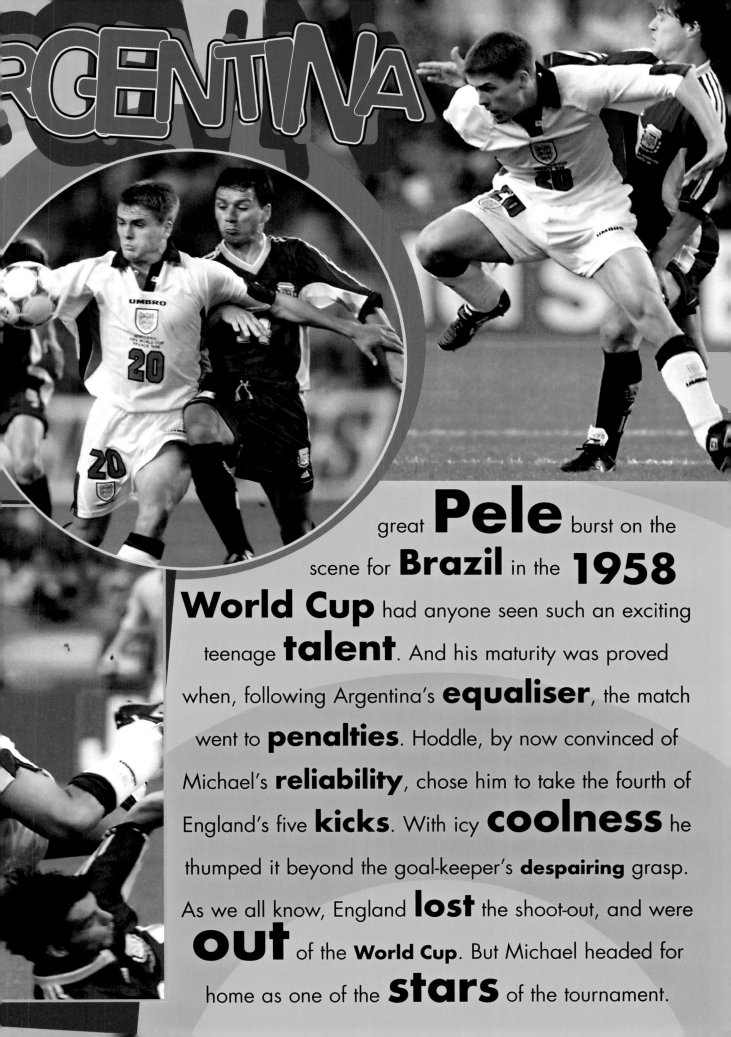

great **Pele** burst on the scene for **Brazil** in the **1958 World Cup** had anyone seen such an exciting teenage **talent**. And his maturity was proved when, following Argentina's **equaliser**, the match went to **penalties**. Hoddle, by now convinced of Michael's **reliability**, chose him to take the fourth of England's five **kicks**. With icy **coolness** he thumped it beyond the goal-keeper's **despairing** grasp. As we all know, England **lost** the shoot-out, and were **out** of the **World Cup**. But Michael headed for home as one of the **stars** of the tournament.

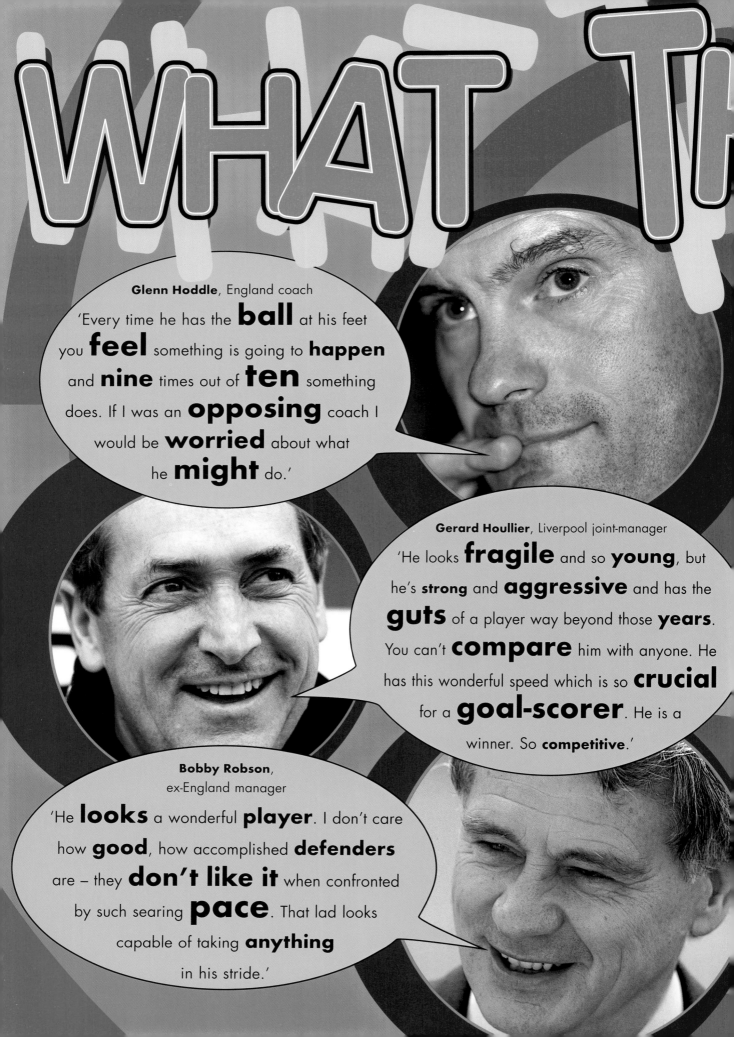

WHAT TH

Glenn Hoddle, England coach

'Every time he has the **ball** at his feet you **feel** something is going to **happen** and **nine** times out of **ten** something does. If I was an **opposing** coach I would be **worried** about what he **might** do.'

Gerard Houllier, Liverpool joint-manager

'He looks **fragile** and so **young**, but he's **strong** and **aggressive** and has the **guts** of a player way beyond those **years**. You can't **compare** him with anyone. He has this wonderful speed which is so **crucial** for a **goal-scorer**. He is a winner. So **competitive**.'

Bobby Robson,
ex-England manager

'He **looks** a wonderful **player**. I don't care how **good**, how accomplished **defenders** are – they **don't like it** when confronted by such searing **pace**. That lad looks capable of taking **anything** in his stride.'

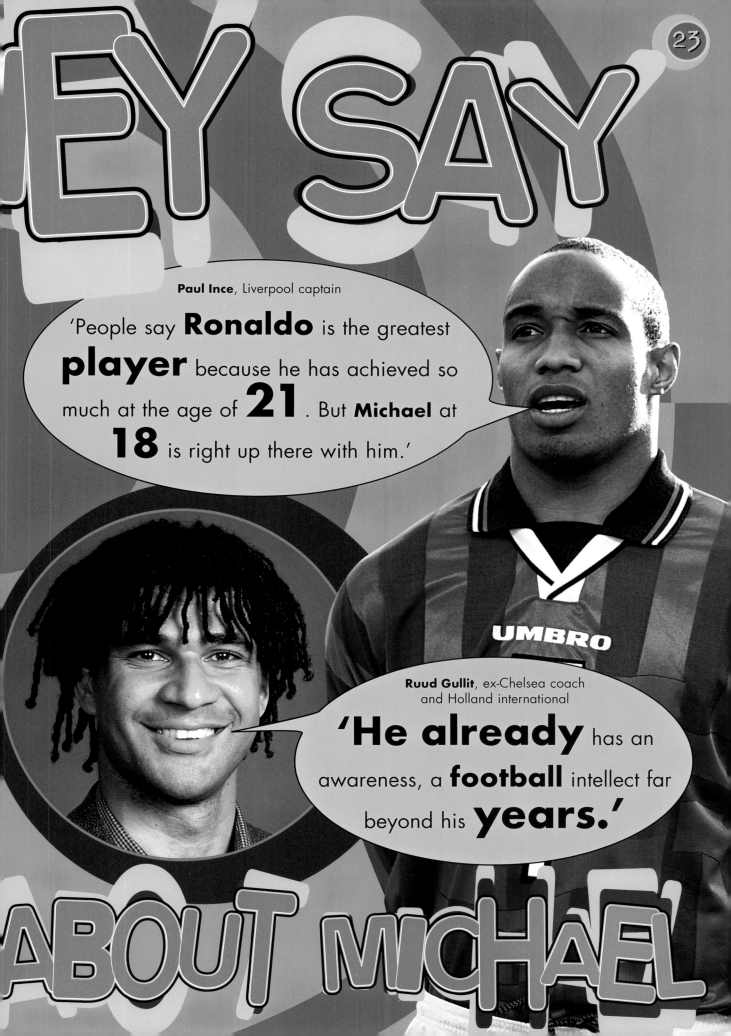

CHARACTER

Despite his status as the **highest-paid teenager** in world **football**, Michael has remained a **modest**, **level-headed** young **man**.

Not for him **flash** nightclubs and pop star friends, Michael **prefers** to live **close** to his **family**, and spends **most** of his time off watching television at **home**. His **friends** are the same ones he made at school. **Success** has **not** changed him. **Michael** also has a **generous** side to his **character**, and he **remembers** those less fortunate than himself. After a **bomb blast** that killed and maimed scores of people in **Omagh**, Northern Ireland in **August 1998**, Michael heard about a young **Liverpool fan** called **Rory McGrory** who had been **seriously injured**. Michael sent him a **message** of **support**, and Rory was promised a **day out** at **Anfield** as soon as he was **well** again.

THE FUTU

Just 10 minutes before **Liverpool's** first home **game** of the 1998/99 season, **Michael** signed a new five-year **contract** pledging his **future** to **The Reds** until **2003**. The deal was worth a reported **£20,000** a week to Michael, guaranteeing him a **fortune** of **£5m** before he turns **23!** And that doesn't **count** all the money he makes from **sponsorship** deals with companies like **Umbro** sportswear and **Tissot** watches. But for Michael, it meant he could **concentrate** on what he **loves** doing best – **playing football** and **scoring goals**. After putting pen to paper he said: 'All I **want** to do is **focus** on my **football** and help bring **more silverware** back to Liverpool. 'Liverpool's joint-manager, **Roy Evans**, was relieved Michael was **staying**. Many of Europe's **richest** clubs, like **Juventus** and **Barcelona**, wanted to buy him.

'**We** are **delighted** he has **signed** for such a **length** of **time,**' said Evans.

Carling **Player** Of The **Year** **1998**

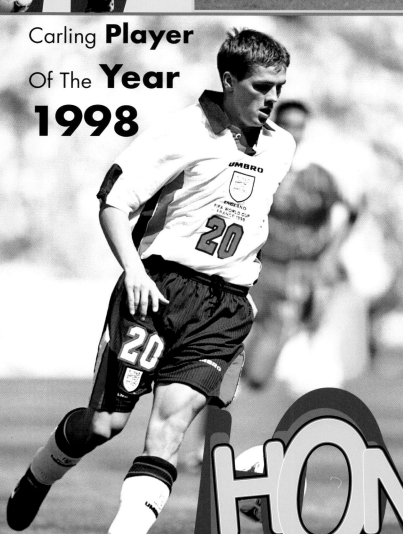

Youngest player ever to score for **Liverpool**

FA Youth Cup winners' medal, **1996**

PFA Young **Player** Of The Year **1998**

HONOURS

Capped at England Under 16, **Under 18**, Under 20 and **Under 21 levels**

Youngest player to **play** for **England** this **century**

Youngest player **ever** to score for **England**

Played first **competitive game**, for Mold Alexandra Under 10s in **August 1987**. Came on as **substitute** and **scored**

Scored his first-ever **hat-trick**, for **Mold Alexandra** against Caergwrle on September 19, **1987**, Ended the **season** in the Clwyd **Junior League** with **34** goals in **28** games

EARLY DAYS

Youngest player to play for **Deeside** Primary Schools, **beating** record set by **Gary Speed** – later a **professional** with **Leeds**, **Everton** and **Newcastle**

Beat Ian Rush's **record goals** in a season for Deeside Primary **Schools**, finishing on **97** in 1990

Beat the England **Schoolboys** goal-scoring **record**, jointly held by **Nick Barmby** and **Kevin Gallen**

Scored all four **goals** for England Under 18s on his **debut** in a **4-0** win against **Northern Ireland** at York City FC

LIVERPOOL CAREER

1996 FA Youth **Cup winners'** medal

First team debut, May 6, 1997 vs **Wimbledon**

1996/97
League appearances **2**, goals **1**

1997/98
League appearances **36**, goals **18**

ENGLAND CAREER

Debut vs **Chile**, February 11, **1998**

International caps **9** (Chile, Switzerland, Portugal, Morocco, Belgium, Tunisia, Romania, Colombia, Argentina) Goals **3**